HOUSE PLANTS

AND THEIR

F*CKED-UP THOUGHTS

HOUSE PLANTS

AND THEIR

F*CKED-UP THOUGHTS

**P.S.,
THEY HATE YOU**

CARLYLE CHRISTOFF
& ELISABETH SAAKE

THE
collective
BOOK STUDIO

CONTENTS

The Popular Crowd

The Drama Queens

The Bitches

THE
POPULAR
CROWD

It's no surprise that everyone
wants them. But do you have what it
takes to keep them satisfied?

Fake Plant

BOTANICUS FAKEROOSKI

I was made in the glory of plant's image: immortal, all-seeing. I'll never die, but neither shall I truly live. I remain stuck in this cursed, halfway purgatory.

◆ WATERING

One time your mom watered me by accident when you were on vacation. It's the only time I've truly felt alive.

☀ LOCATION

Anywhere you like, including in the fish tank.

SAGITTARIUS

NOT EDIBLE.
So very not edible.

You want me; I can see it in your eyes. But I'm a lot to handle. My needs can't be met by just anyone. Find a fake plant from Pottery Barn if you won't put in the work.

WATERING

Exactly twenty drops of water from an eyedropper daily, delivered in a perfect circle around my base. Not nineteen. Twenty.

LOCATION

Place me next to the window, where I can flex on your neighbor.

VIRGO

EDIBLE.
But not exactly "yum."

Fiddle-Leaf Fig

FICUS LYRATA

Golden Pothos

EPIPREMNUM AUREUM

Some refer to me as Golden Pothos, but I prefer Devil's Ivy because of my devil-may-care attitude. For example, I don't care if you leave and never, ever come back.

💧 **WATERING**
Sing to me in dulcet tones while watering . . . in Celtic.

☀ **LOCATION**
Where I cascade like a green waterfall.

GEMINI

NOT EDIBLE.
Don't do it. Eat something from the fridge instead. Maybe hummus?

I kindly request that you relocate me from your master bathroom. Yes, the light and humidity are just right, but all those folds are more than I can handle. The bloom is off the rose, my dear. I'm a plant, so I should know.

💧 **WATERING**
We can't talk watering until you remove me from this trashy plastic pot.

☀ **LOCATION**
Somewhere I can coil, climb, and judge you mercilessly from above.

CAPRICORN

NOT EDIBLE.
Unless you're already dead and want to stay that way.

Heartleaf Philodendron

PHILODENDRON HEDERACEUM

Jade Plant

CRASSULA OVATA

I understand that you are considering taking up bonsai. Before you start snipping at me, however, may I suggest other possible hobbies? Skydiving? Rock climbing? Long walks on short piers?

💧 **WATERING**

Stop sticking your finger in my soil to test my moisture. That's rude!

☀ **LOCATION**

The spot by the fireplace looks nice. But no fires, please. That's the price you pay for my happiness.

VIRGO

NOT EDIBLE.
Stop reaching for me.

17

Just between you and me, I am not really bamboo and there isn't anything about me that is actually lucky, as you may have noticed. As a matter of fact, I'm a fraud. Not as big a fraud as your father the bank embezzler, but still pretty big. That must have been pretty embarrassing for you, by the way.

💧 **WATERING**
Every two weeks, one teaspoon of Lucky Lager with the H2O, pretty please.

☀ **LOCATION**
I like things shady. Like your boyfriend.

GEMINI

NOT EDIBLE.
Give it a try though. You might get lucky. Or not.

Lucky Bamboo

DRACAENA SANDERIANA

Majesty Palm

RAVENEA RIVULARIS

As I reach toward the light
to beautify your home,
it's hard for me to feel as
majestic as nature intended
with you bingeing on
cheese puffs and reality TV
in your underwear.

WATERING
Gently spray me with mineral water from a
silver mister, daily.

☀ **LOCATION**
On a hilltop with sweeping views of my
kingdom. OK, the floor is fine. Sigh.

LEO

EDIBLE.
*Though all that majesty
might be hard to digest.*

Thank you so much for braiding my trunks together. That is so very charming. Now if you could just figure out how to give my leaves a perm, we could complete my makeover from "plant" to "low-budget movie star."

🌢 **WATERING**

Drink the excess water in my saucer to prove that you love me. The browner the better. You've been there.

☀ **LOCATION**

Right next to the front door, where I can make the guests feel insecure.

SAGITTARIUS

EDIBLE.

My nuts are edible. I'm serious. Taste 'em.

Money Tree Plant

PACHIRA AQUATICA

Peace Lily

SPATHIPHYLLUM

24

I've taken lots of deep breaths while thinking about this. I'm turning toward the sunlight and vibrating with the universe over here, but it must be said: that prissy fern in her fancy-ass pot on her little stand in a goddamn sunbeam is really fucking with my flow. Ditch that skanky bitch immediately. Namaste.

💧 **WATERING**

I prefer dew collected from high-altitude mountain grass. And no, I don't mean the mountain dew you distill behind the shed.

☀ **LOCATION**

I. Just. Need. One. Moment. Of. Quiet. Is that too much to ask?!

LIBRA

NOT EDIBLE.
Very NOT edible.

If it's the Luck of the Irish to be left abandoned and shriveling on the back porch, then, hooray, I won the lottery.

💧 **WATERING**
Aquafina—with just a hint of the old Bushmills—will do the trick.

☀ **LOCATION**
Place me high, so your kids stop trying to yank off "lucky clovers"!

LIBRA

NOT EDIBLE.
Or "eatable" if you don't know what "edible" means.

Purple Shamrock

OXALIS TRIANGULARIS

Snake Plant

SANSEVIERIA

Did you know that one of the many health benefits I bring to your home is that I filter toxins and purify your air? But even on my best day I can't handle your cheap perfume or the pungent odor of your desperation.

💧 **WATERING**
Hiss while you water me.

☀ **LOCATION**
Tuck me where the sun don't shine. And no, I didn't mean "there," which is already fully occupied by your head.

SCORPIO

NOT EDIBLE.
Skull and crossbones, baby.

Dainty green pearls adorn my delicate stems like jewels. I spill gracefully from my planter, stretching my glistening tendrils toward the . . . wait, what? A Formica countertop?! The shame!

💧 **WATERING**

Please say "I am a cloud, and I giveth gentle rains unto you" before each watering session.

☀ **LOCATION**

Draped dramatically across your heaving bosom. No? Fine, window ledge.

LIBRA

NOT EDIBLE.

Order takeout. Perhaps pho from that one place?

String of Pearls

SENECIO ROWLEYANUS

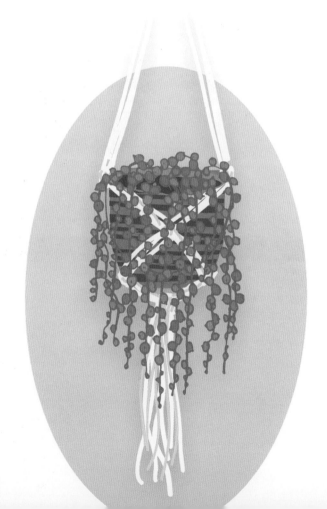

Swiss Cheese Plant

MONSTERA DELICIOSA

Just to be clear, I am named for the glorious perforations in my leaves that look a bit like the holes in Swiss cheese, and not for a smell that I emit. You, however, might want to get yourself checked out. I don't really mind, but the other plants are starting to complain.

💧 **WATERING**
Please use a tea kettle. I like Earl Grey.

☀ **LOCATION**
Place me in your kitchen, where I can watch you make unpalatable Thai food for the seven millionth time.

AQUARIUS

NOT EDIBLE.
I wouldn't. And no, my leaves don't actually taste like cheese.

33

Does my shape remind you of a palm tree gently swaying above the white sands of a Hawaiian beach? Perhaps you should just go for it and book yourself a trip to the islands. You deserve it! Get a one-way ticket though. No need to rush back.

💧 **WATERING**
Undistilled water? Yuck.

☀ **LOCATION**
In any room that your trunk-scratching cat is not allowed to enter.

PISCES

NOT EDIBLE.
Not a great idea. As if you've ever had one.

Yucca

YUCCA ELEPHANTIPES

ZZ Plant

ZAMIOCULCAS ZAMIIFOLIA

I am about as easygoing a plant friend as you can imagine. I always look good; just hit me with the water when you have the time. I'm chill. Fire up that bong, too, brother. I dig it.

💧 **WATERING**
Whenever you have a chance. I'm good.

☀ **LOCATION**
Totally good right here. Or there. Whatever.

♓
PISCES

NOT EDIBLE.
"Not" with a capital N.

THE DRAMA QUEENS

The misfits, rebels, and renegades are here to tell you what they think. They're not miserable, just misunderstood.

Air Plant

TILLANDSIA IONANTHA

Do you have any idea how many nutrients most plants guzzle down on the daily? Then they wonder why they hardly fit in their pots. Gross. I drank three calories by accident last week and I've been trying to throw up ever since.

💧 **WATERING**
No. Just no. Air is my water.

☀ **LOCATION**
Dangling on fishing line from a hook in your hideous popcorn ceiling.

GEMINI

NOT EDIBLE.
Uh, no. Maybe you should just stick with Taco Bell, tubby.

You thought a cactus would be hard to kill, right? Let my desiccated corpse serve as a brittle reminder of your ineptitude.

💧 **WATERING**
Go easy. Think "desert." Don't get that confused with "dessert," either.

☀ **LOCATION**
Please put me in a high-traffic zone, where I can do damage.

ARIES

EDIBLE.
You might consider removing the spines first. Or not. Whatever floats your boat.

Angel Wings Cactus

OPUNTA ALBISPINA

Basil

OCIMUM BASILICUM

For all your excited talk about a Pesto Party, I can't see myself ending up on your plate. You are more likely to buy your pesto in a can, along with cut-rate vino and pre-sliced American cheese. Keeping it classy, as usual.

💧 **WATERING**

Let's avoid waiting until I keel over. I am not a dried herb.

☀️ **LOCATION**

In your sunny kitchen window, with all the other potted herbs denied the bliss of outdoor soil.

TAURUS

EDIBLE.

Duh. If you didn't know, maybe you should complete that associate's degree, Einstein.

45

I generally thrive in the tropics and prefer high humidity. Lucky for me, I live with a bunch of mouth-breathers.

💧 **WATERING**

Can you play the harp and water me at the same time? I mean the big harp, not the little one.

☀ **LOCATION**

In your bedroom. I could use a hearty laugh.

CAPRICORN

NOT EDIBLE.
But, my cousin the pineapple is. Second cousin, once removed, actually.

46

Bromeliad Guzmania

BROMELIACEAE

47

Dragon Tree

DRACAENA MARGINATA

Dude, I'm aware of your creepy dragon obsession and that dungeon game you play. But I'm not an actual dragon. Get a life.

💧 **WATERING**
I can tolerate erratic watering—but try to get your act together.

☀ **LOCATION**
In a bright spot, as far as possible from your coat of arms and coveted canvas of a damsel in distress.

SCORPIO

NOT EDIBLE.
Can't add dragon magic to potions. Stop trying.

Frizzle Sizzle? Really? Please tell me I was named by Snoop Dogg. That's the only plausible explanation.

💧 WATERING

You just do your best. I know you're not capable of much, other than eating 15 Butterfinger minis in one sitting.

☀ LOCATION

In a sunny window or balcony, but don't overdo the "sizzle."

LEO

NOT EDIBLE.

Try lettuce instead. That's also a plant, but it tastes good and won't make you die.

Frizzle Sizzle

ALBUCA SPIRALIS

Giant Bird of Paradise

STRELITZIA NICOLAI

I'm a bird of paradise. Emphasis on "paradise." Not the bird of some dump with wall-to-wall shag carpeting. It's mortifying. Set me free.

💧 **WATERING**
Please hire staff to water me correctly. You can't manage it.

☀ **LOCATION**
In your brightest bathroom. (Please use the room sparingly or not at all. Get a bucket.)

LEO

NOT EDIBLE.
I'm offended. How did this even cross your mind? Not all birds are chicken.

To say you're overwatering me is an understatement. My pot looks like a Louisiana bayou minus the alligators and moonshiners. What about "cactus" don't you understand?

💧 **WATERING**
Easy does it, cowgirl.

☀️ **LOCATION**
You would think as a cactus that I love sun. . . . But guess again!

ARIES

NOT EDIBLE.
As edible as a soggy pin cushion.

Moon Cactus

GYMNOCALYCIUM MIHANOVICHII

Nerve Plant

FITTONIA VERSHAFFELTII

THE DRAMA QUEENS

I am referred to as a nerve plant because my elegantly lined foliage looks like the many-veined nervous system. I don't actually have nerves. However, if I did, your singing would be getting on my very last one, and that's for damn sure.

💧 **WATERING**
Water me, but don't fucking touch me.

☀ **LOCATION**
By the jar of liquid plant food (hint, hint!).

AQUARIUS

NOT EDIBLE.
But, sure . . . If you don't mind seeing fairies with magic wands floating about.

I know my foliage looks like gorgeous flowing locks, but please stop with the facial cutouts of Taylor Swift. That is not OK, and you are not OK.

💧 **WATERING**
A spray bottle, a comb, and a scoop of hair gel, please.

☀ **LOCATION**
A south-facing window. Natural light brings out my highlights.

ARIES

NOT EDIBLE.
Ewww. Not with that mouth. I just threw up a little.

Ponytail Palm

BEAUCARNEA RECURVATA

Rubber Plant

FICUS ELASTICA

Remember the song about the ant with "high apple pie in the sky hopes" who tries to move the rubber tree plant? Such determination. That ant accomplishes the impossible. Speaking of ants, can you zap any you see near me? Go heavy. No survivors.

RUBBER PLANT

💧 **WATERING**
When you stop being self-obsessed, maybe you can think of me and my needs.

☀ **LOCATION**
Anywhere you like. I am here to dazzle and delight.

♌
LEO

NOT EDIBLE.
And why won't you just eat normal stuff? WTF?

What do I think about you?
Not much, to be honest. You're
just another human crawling
around on this planet, stealing
my water and sunshine. I hope
you weren't looking for love and
encouragement. So far, it's been
two years of the silent treatment
between us. Why break our
glorious streak?

💧 **WATERING**
Only the finest Junmai Daiginjo sake, please.

☀ **LOCATION**
I don't care where, just pick a spot and stop
moving me around every time you're looking
for your vape.

SCORPIO

NOT EDIBLE.
*Does it physically hurt to be
that stupid? I hope you don't
procreate.*

Sago Palm

CYCAS REVOLUTA

Spider Plant

CHLOROPHYTUM COMOSUM

I am named a "spider plant" because some think I resemble an arachnid. I find this troubling, as we all know spiders are aggressive and gruesome creatures that elicit terror. I am lovely and kind, with not a cruel bone in my body. However, if I were a spider I would web you up tight and suck every ounce of life out of your body. But I'm totally not a spider . . . I'm as harmless as they come.

💧 **WATERING**
I like my water with a twist of lime.

☀ **LOCATION**
Perhaps in the den. Please close the door behind you as you leave.

SCORPIO

EDIBLE.
But don't overdo it. I tend to bite back.

I know you want to experience the "great circle of life," but I think you need more help than I can provide, my friend. I generally tackle two, maybe three flies a month. Maybe take out the trash every once in a while?

💧 **WATERING**
If I'm dry, no eatey fly.

☀️ **LOCATION**
In the kitchen at twilight, with windows open and the lights on.

SCORPIO

NOT EDIBLE.
What part of "vulnerable species" do you not understand?

Venus Fly Trap

DIONAEA MUSCIPULA

THE
BITCHES

These bitchin' botanicals are thirsty, basic, and looking for attention. But be forewarned: They'll steal your man, they'll steal your thunder, and they'll somehow leave you wanting more.

Aloe Vera

ALOE BARBADENSIS MILLER

I am cool, calm, and collected, baby. Treat me right, and my gel will not only heal your body, but my presence will rejuvenate your soul. I also work really well as lube. Just sayin'.

💧 **WATERING**
I like it wet.

☀ **LOCATION**
On the bedside table where you hide your "personal massager."

🦀
CANCER

NOT EDIBLE.
You wish, pal.

I can go on and on about Boston. The lobster rolls, the marathon, Fenway Park, and heavily accented people saying "Christiner" instead of "Christina." But there is so much more to the city than that. There's also the baked beans. OK, I think that covers it, actually.

💧 **WATERING**

Before watering, please yell, "Norm!" like Sam from *Cheers*.

☀ **LOCATION**

Hang me high in a basket, where I can safely make fun of your stupid cat.

LIBRA

EDIBLE.

Get that bib on and give it a go. You never know.

Boston Fern

NEPHROLEPIS EXALTATA

Catnip

NEPETA CATARIA

I'm fine with a little nibble now and then, but things are getting weird. Your cat is exhibiting addictive tendencies, and I'm starting to fear for my life.

◆ **WATERING**
Fill my bowl while I pretend not to care.

☀ **LOCATION**
On a sunlit perch where I can view my domain. Between naps.

| ♉ **TAURUS** | **EDIBLE.**
Take a nibble. Meow. |

Did you know that my species grows naturally along the base of the Himalayas? My ancestors witnessed intrepid humans risk dangerous ascents to surmount those glorious icy peaks. I, on the other hand, get to watch you struggle on the StairMaster and then complain endlessly about your sore glutes.

💧 **WATERING**

Keep me wet. However, I am guessing that might be difficult.

☀ **LOCATION**

Anywhere that pleases you. No, not there. Or there. Try again.

CAPRICORN

EDIBLE.

Grab a plate and that Thousand Island dressing, fancy pants.

Coin Plant

PILEA PEPEROMIOIDES

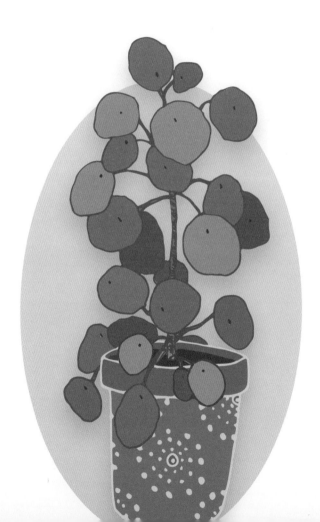

Elephant Ears Plant

COLOCASIA GIGANTEAN

Stand back everyone, Big Daddy is here, and this joint is now officially mine. I own this room and everything in it, and I will never forget or forgive a mistake. So get your A-game on, and let's get down to focusing on my needs right now.

💧 **WATERING**
Bring a hose.

☀ **LOCATION**
On your shaded patio, where I will flourish and become king of your miniature jungle.

LEO

EDIBLE.
But, only if cooked first, or you are in for some pain . . . not that you don't deserve that.

Although I'm a notorious thriver and very hardy, even I have my limits. News flash: Plants need water, even if just occasionally. Setting my own needs aside for a minute, though, I think you really need to feed your goldfish. This joint is a death trap.

WATERING

I prefer dry martinis with no garnish, three times a week. Top shelf, please.

LOCATION

Hang me from a basket or let me climb a trellis. No matter. I will eventually take over the whole joint.

AQUARIUS

NOT EDIBLE.
No means no.

English Ivy

HEDERA HELIX

81

Heart Hoya

HOYA KERRII

It seems the heart shape of my leaves has made me seem a clever Valentine's Day gift for your lover. Think again, Romeo. Word to the wise: Jewelry.

💧 **WATERING**
If you put a saucer under my pot, we could avoid these embarrassing accidents.

☀ **LOCATION**
In the solarium that you need to build for me.

LIBRA

EDIBLE.
But again, there are better options.

Yes, my name does indeed sound like a bad 1970s porn movie. Really, though, I am beautiful and sophisticated, hard to fathom yet extremely satisfying . . . like an '80s porn movie. How do I know all this? Because your husband watches the stuff on the big screen the very second you leave the house for any reason ever.

💧 **WATERING**
Shimmy before me, as if you, yourself, were the falling rain.

☀ **LOCATION**
Make me the centerpiece of your charmingly retro patio tiki bar.

SCORPIO

EDIBLE.
No toxic effects have been reported from eating me. But, of course, dead men tell no tales.

Jungle Velvet

CALATHEA WARSCEWICZII

Key Lime Tree

CITRUS AURANTIIFOLIA

I know you've been longing to make a delicious key lime pie. Not gonna happen unless your husband stops raiding my branches for late-night Cuba libres to take the edge off the tedium of his pointless life. The boredom thing is probably your fault, though, so no pie for you.

💧 **WATERING**
No water, no limes. Set a reminder.

☀ **LOCATION**
I just love it out here on your deck, where I can pretend I'm in actual nature.

TAURUS

EDIBLE.
Well of course my fruits are edible. And I love that face you make when you take a bite.

I prefer my fruit to dangle until it drops off naturally. But, if you must use me, perhaps a delicate merengue or a creamy custard? If you even think about stripping me bare for your little delinquent's lemonade stand again, I'm gonna lose it.

💧 **WATERING**

Water me thorough and water me deep. Make my roots curl or no lemons for you.

☀ **LOCATION**

On your back deck where I can catch some rays. Please keep the door closed.

VIRGO

EDIBLE.

Yes, lemons are edible, idiot. Did you know that they are also a little sour?

Meyer Lemon Tree

CITRUS MEYERI

Moth Orchid

PHALAENOPSIS ORCHID

Please stop looking at me like that. It's not my fault I was chosen by your mother-in-law. I'll just sit here blooming my heart out until my flowers wither and you throw me in the trash like a cheap bouquet. Completely heartless, just like your mother-in-law is always whispering.

💧 **WATERING**
If you are going to continue with unfiltered, don't bother.

☀ **LOCATION**
In the center of the fancy dining room table, where you don't eat; next to the candles you don't light.

SAGITTARIUS

EDIBLE.
But not famously delicious.

91

Make way, please, I'm strutting my stuff over here. Have you ever seen foliage as big and lush as mine? Stop pretending you don't find me attractive. I'm irresistible, and we both know it.

🌢 WATERING

Whisper "gentle waterfall, gentle waterfall" over and over while you shower me with affection.

☀ LOCATION

Directly in front of your largest mirror. Damn, I look good.

LEO

NOT EDIBLE.
What!? Why!?

Peacock Plant

CALATHEA MAKOYANA

Prayer Plant

MARANTA LEUCONEURA

In the evening, you may notice that my leaves fold up a bit—as if I am in prayer. Don't mind me, I'm just praying for your soul, heathen. Do you feel the flames of hell licking at your ankles? My mind is a crystal pool. Ommmmmm.

💧 **WATERING**
I pray for rain. From you. Please water me.

☀ **LOCATION**
The physical world is beneath me.

SAGITTARIUS

NOT EDIBLE.
Just breathe me in.

Look, I know I said some plants in this book are edible, but I'm no botanist. I've killed every plant I've ever owned, and I'd hate to accidentally kill you, too. So, don't eat the plants and don't sue me if you do. This sentence will be exhibit A in any future trial.

Library of Congress Cataloging-in-Publication Data available.

ISBN: 978-1-951412-03-6
Ebook ISBN: 978-1-951412-70-8
LCCN: 2022938295

Printed using Forest Stewardship Council certified stock from
sustainably managed forests.

Manufactured in China.

Design and typesetting by AJ Hansen.
Illustrations by Shutterstock.

3 5 7 9 10 8 6 4 2

The Collective Book Studio®
Oakland, California
www.thecollectivebook.studio